D0438227

FLY GUY PRESENTS: SCARY CREATURES!

5 BOOKZZZ IN 1!

Tedd Arnold

Scholastic Inc.

To my pal Brady —T.A.
For my pal Wyatt—T.A.
For Dr. Margaret (Canopy Meg) Lowman, biologist, explorer, educator, ecologist, and fellow Elmiran!—T.A.
To Caroline Van Kirk Bissell, the "Bat Lady" of the Chautauqua Bird, Tree & Garden Club—T.A.
For Judy and Gary, who have many snake stories to tell!—T.A.
Thank you, Sara Ruane, for your contributions to this book—T.A.

Photos ©: cover top background: Ludmila Ivashchenko/Shutterstock; cover top left: Michael Durham/age fotostock; cover top right: reptiles4all/Shutterstock; cover bottom left: Violetastock/Getty Images; cover bottom right: Roger Harris/Science Source; back cover: Cindy Creighton/Shutterstock; 5: Stephen Frink/Getty Images; 10-11: Audubon Nature Institute; 12 top: strmko/iStockphoto; 12 center: FAUP/Shutterstock; 12 bottom: divejunkie/iStockphoto; 13 top left: Ginet -Drin/age fotostock; 13 top right: Dan Burton/age fotostock; 13 center: SeaPics.com; 13 bottom: W. Scott/Shutterstock; 14-15: SeaPics.com; 15 top right: SeaPics.com; 16 bottom: Carlos Villoch/age fotostock; 17 top: Jim Agronick/Shutterstock; 17 bottom: SeaPics.com; 18 top: SeaPics.com; 18 bottom: SeaPics.com; 19 top: Andy Murch/Vwpics/Newscom; 19 bottom: MP cz/Shutterstock; 20-21: Willyam Bradberry/Shutterstock; 22: Tammy616/iStockphoto; 23 top: Bill Curtsinger/National Geographic Creative; 23 bottom: Jurgen Freund/NPL/Minden Pictures; 24 top: Dray van Beeck/Shutterstock; 24 bottom: SeaPics.com; 25 top: demarfa/iStockphoto; 25 center: SeaPics.com; 25 bottom: SeaPics.com; 26 top: SeaPics.com; 26-27: Lawrence Cruciana/Shutterstock; 27 bottom: troischats/iStockphoto; 28 top: SeaPics.com; 28 bottom: SeaPics.com; 29: Reinhard Dirscherl/age fotostock; 30 top: Stuart Keasley/age fotostock; 30-31: Marevision/Getty Images; 32-33: Reinhard Dirscherl/Alamy Stock Photo; 34 top: David Doubilet/National Geographic Creative; 34 bottom: Yasumasa Kobayashi/Nature Production/Minden Pictures; 35 top: Jason Edwards/National Geographic Creative; 35 bottom: Doug Perrine/Nature Picture Library; 36 top: Norbert Probst/imageb/age fotostock; 36 bottom: SeaPics.com; 37: Bill Curtsinger/National Geographic Creative; 39 center: Marques/Shutterstock; 39 background: Wouter Tolenaars/Shutterstock; 44-45: Purcell Team/Alamy Stock Photo; 46: Gary Hincks/Science Source; 47 map: Planetary Visions Ltd/Science Source; 48 left: Walter Myers/Media Bakery; 48 right: Kim Taylor/Warren Photographic/Science Source; 49 top: Roger Harris/Science Photo Library/Corbis; 49 bottom: Andrea Ferrari/NHPA/Photoshot/Science Source; 50 top left: Ohmega1982/iStockphoto; 50 top center: Chris Mattison/Getty Images; 50 top right: GLobalP/iStockphoto; 50 center: Mark Boulton/Alamy Stock Photo; 50 bottom left: Wedekiba/Dreamstime; 50 bottom right: Ken Cavanagh/Alamy Stock Photo; 51 top left: London Taxidermy/Media Bakery; 51 top right: Psihoyos Photography; 51 bottom: John Kaprielian/Science Source; 52 top left: Psihoyos Photography; 52 top right: Sinclair Stammers/Science Source; 52 top right inset: Millard H. Sharp/Science Source; 52 bottom: Marka/Superstock, Inc.; 53: Ken Lucas/Getty Images; 54 top: Craig Brown/Stocktrek Images/Corbis; 54 bottom: Scott Camazine/Science Source; 55 top: NHPA/Superstock, Inc.; 55 bottom: Leonello Calvetti/Science Photo Library/Corbis; 56 top: Stocktrek Images, Inc./Alamy Stock Photo; 56 bottom: Gabbro/Alamy Stock Photo; 57: Psihoyos Photography; 58: Daniel Eskridge/Stocktrek Images/Getty Images; 59 top: The Natural History Museum, London UK/The Image Works; 59 bottom: Craig Brown/Stocktrek Images/Corbis; 60-61: Craig Brown/Stocktrek Images/Corbis; 61 top right: Aaron Amat/Shutterstock; 62 top: Image Source/Getty Images; 62 bottom: Friedrich Saurer/Science Source; 63: Roger Harris/Science Source; 64-65: Victor de Schwanberg/Alamy Stock Photo; 65 bottom right: Hans Strand/Getty Images; 66 top: Psihoyos Photography; 66 bottom: Biosphoto/Superstock, Inc.; 67 top left: Marcel Clemens/Shutterstock; 67 top right: Psihoyos Photography; 67 bottom: Linda Bucklin/Shutterstock; 68 top: Pascal Goetgheluck/Science Source; 68 bottom: Annie Griffiths Belt/National Geographic Creative; 69 top: Corbis/VCG/Getty Images; 69 bottom: Psihoyos Photography; 70: James Leynse/Getty Images; 71 left: Benedictus/Shutterstock; 71 right: Smithsonian Institute/Science Source; 73 bee: Joel Sartore/National Geographic Creative; 73 ant: DrPAS/iStockphoto; 73 ant hill: PeterTG/iStockphoto; 73 right: Salvatore Volpes/iStockphoto; 73 background: elenavolkova/iStockphoto; 78-79 background: Marcin Okupniak/Dreamstime; 80 map: Cartesia/Getty Images; 80 wood frame: Tadeusz Ibrom/Dreamstime; 80-81 background: Nils Weymann/Dreamstime; 81 top: Specker, Donald/Animals Animals; 81 center: CathyKeifer/iStockphoto; 81 bottom: Wild & Natural/Animals Animals; 82-83 background: 1000 Words/Shutterstock; 83 top left: Photo Researchers/Getty Images; 83 top right: DEA Picture Library/Getty Images; 83 bottom left: francesco de marco/Shutterstock; 83 bottom right: johan63/iStockphoto; 84 top: fiulo/iStockphoto; 84 bottom: Wechsler, Doug/Animals Animals; 85 eggs: Perennou Nuridsany/Science Source; 85 larvae: smuay/iStockphoto; 85 pupa: Perennou Nuridsany/Science Source; 85 adult: Nigel Cattlin/Science Source; 85 aphid: Bartomeu Borrell/Media Bakery; 86 top: Cindy Creighton/Shutterstock; 86-87 background: chudoba/Shutterstock; 87 top: skynetphoto/Shutterstock; 87 bottom: Beneda Miroslav/Shutterstock; 88 top: Tokle/iStockphoto; 88 bottom: Wild & Natural/Animals Animals; 88-89 background: Chunli Li/Dreamstime; 90 top left: Minden Pictures/Superstock, Inc.; 90 top right: Steve Gschmeissner/Science Source; 90 bottom left: hnijjar007/iStockphoto; 90 bottom right: Gewoldi/iStockphoto; 91 top left: Hans Lang/Corbis Images; 91 top right: Charles Krebs/Getty Images; 91 bottom: Alex Wild Photography; 92 left: ntzolov/iStockphoto; 92 right: tzooka/iStockphoto; 92-93 background: Krasnevsky/iStockphoto; 93 top: Pat Morris/Ardea; 93 bottom: Barnaby Chambers/Shutterstock; 94 top: Paul Reeves Photography/Shutterstock; 94 bottom: Katarina Christenson/Shutterstock; 94-95 background top: Johannesk/Dreamstime; 94-95 background bottom: Opas Chotiphantawanon/Shutterstock; 95 left: Clark, Jack/Animals Animals; 95 right: Specker, Donald/Animals Animals; 96: huePhotography/iStockphoto; 97 top: ivkuzmin/iStockphoto; 97 center: John Clegg/Ardea; 97 bottom: Piotr Naskrecki/Minden Pictures; 98 top: Reyes Garcia III/USDA; 98 bottom left: Rolf Nussbaumer/imageBROKER/age fotostock; 98 bottom right: Peter Macdiarmid/Reuters/Newscom; 98 background: mexrix/Shutterstock; 99 top: Jan Luit/Minden Pictures; 99 center: Ardea/Morris, Pat/Animals Animals; 99 background: mexrix/Shutterstock; 100 center: Tomatito/Shutterstock; 101-102 background: Johannes Kornelius/Shutterstock; 101 top: Pascal Goetgheluck/Ardea; 102 left: tunart/iStockphoto; 102 right: Minden Pictures/Superstock, Inc.; 103: Michele Menegon/Ardea; 104 left: Ratchapol Yindeesuk/Shutterstock; 104 right: Gavriel Jecan/Media Bakery; 104-105 background: Pasticcio/iStockphoto; 105 left: Chappell, Mark/Animals Animals; 105 right: Ardea/Sailer, Steffen & Alexandra/Animals Animals; 106: teo73/iStockphoto; 107: Yuzo Nakagawa/Minden Pictures; 112-113 background: Brad Williams Photography; 114: Mattias Klum/National Geographic Creative; 115 top left: Michael Durham/Minden Pictures; 115 top right: Merlin D. Tuttle/Science Source; 115 bottom left: Design Pics/Media Bakery; 115 bottom right: JohnPitcher/iStockphoto; 116 top left: Kptan123/iStockphoto; 116 top right: Pat Morris/Ardea; 116 bottom: Merlin Tuttle/Science Source; 117: Ivan Kuzmin/Shutterstock; 118 top left: Jason Edwards/National Geographic Creative; 118 top center: Mark Bowler/Science Source; 118 top right: B.G. Thomson/Science Source; 118 center: ER Degginger/Science Source; 118 bottom: FrankRamspott/iStockphoto; 119 top : OndrejVladyka/iStockphoto; 119 bottom: jasantiso/iStockphoto; 120: Super Prin/Shutterstock; 121: Stephen Belcher/Minden Pictures; 122 top: Joe McDonald/Visuals Unlimited; 122 bottom left: Wil Meinderts, Buiten-beeld/Minden Pictures; 122 bottom right: the4js /iStockphoto; 123: Nature Picture Library/Alamy Stock Photo; 124 top : Mark Bowler/Science Source; 124 bottom: Dr. Merlin D. Tuttle/Science Source; 125 top: Tim Laman/National Geographic Creative; 125 bottom: Mealmeaw/Dreamstime; 126 left: Merlin D. Tuttle/Science Source; 126 right: Merlin D. Tuttle/Science Source; 127 top left: Michael Rolands/Shutterstock; 127 top right: Merlin D. Tuttle/Science Source; 127 bottom: Nick Gordon/Ardea/Animals Animals; 128 top : Dave Roberts/Science Source; 128 bottom: ARCO/Braun, C/age fotostock; 129 left: Merlin Tuttle/BCI/Science Source; 129 right: Michael Fogden/Animals Animals; 130 top left: Christian Ziegler/Minden Pictures; 130 top right: Christian Ziegler/Minden Pictures; 130 bottom: Lynn Johnson/National Geographic Creative; 131 top: Stephen Dalton/Science Source; 131 bottom: Isselee/Dreamstime; 132-133: Michael Durham/Minden Pictures; 134: Chien Lee/Minden Pictures; 135 top : Stephen Dalton/Minden Pictures; 135 bottom: John Serrao/Science Source; 136 top: Dr. Merlin D. Tuttle/Bat Conservation International/Science Source; 136 bottom: Dr. Merlin D. Tuttle/Bat Conservation International/Science Source; 137 top left: ER Degginger/Science Source; 137 top right: Roland Seitre/Minden Pictures; 137 bottom: Dr. Merlin D. Tuttle/Bat Conservation International/Science Source; 138: Merlin D. Tuttle/Science Source; 139: Christian Ziegler/Getty Images; 141: Biosphoto/Superstock, Inc.; 146-147 background: Rob Hainer/Shutterstock; 148 top left: Jack Goldfarb/Media Bakery; 148 top right: Chaitud Pongthanaiporn/Dreamstime; 148 center: Danun13/Dreamstime; 148 bottom: Greg Dale/National Geographic Creative; 149: Stefan Schierle/Fotolia; 150 top: Dr. Tim Davenport/WCS; 150 bottom: luther2k/Fotolia; 151 left: bitis73/iStockphoto; 151 right: John Cancalosi/Ardea; 152 top left: Courtesy of Sara Ruane; 152 top center left: Dennis Donohue/Dreamstime; 152 top center right: Shannon Plummer/iStockphoto; 152 top right: skynavin/iStockphoto; 152 center top: Courtesy of Sara Ruane; 152 center bottom left: the4js/iStockphoto; 152 center bottom right: Courtesy of Sara Ruane; 152 bottom: FrankRamspott/iStockphoto; 153 top left: Twildlife/Dreamstime; 153 top right: Kitto Studio/Shutterstock; 153 bottom: Paul Sutherland/National Geographic Creative; 154: Matthijs Kuijpers/Dreamstime; 155: Design Pics/Media Bakery; 156: pitchwayz/iStockphoto; 157 top left: Rujitop/iStockphoto; 157 top right: benzinefoto/iStockphoto; 157 bottom: Lightwriter1949/iStockphoto; 158 top: Paul & Joyce/Animals Animals; 158 bottom: Kevin & Suzette Hanley/Animals Animals; 159 top left: alptraum/iStockphoto; 159 top right: ZiZ7StockPhotos/Shutterstock; 159 bottom: Narcis Parfenti/Shutterstock; 160 top: Pat Canova/Alamy Stock Photo; 160 bottom: MR1805/iStockphoto; 161 top: Ingo Arndt/Minden Pictures/National Geographic Creative; 161 bottom: Nicolas Perrault III/Wikimedia; 162 top: Duncan Usher/age fotostock; 162 bottom: Animals Animals/Superstock, Inc.; 163 left: Michael Fogden/Animals Animals; 163 right: Mc Donald Wildlife Photog./Animals Animals; 164 top: Mark Kostich/iStockphoto; 164 bottom: Andrew Bee/Getty Images; 165 top: reptiles4all/Shutterstock; 165 bottom left: LittleStocker/Shutterstock; 165 bottom right: mark higgins/Shutterstock; 166: Zigmund Leszczynski/Animals Animals; 167 top: Paul Freed/Animals Animals; 167 bottom: ER Degginger/Science Source; 168: Pete Oxford/Getty Images; 169: David M. Dennis/Animals Animals; 170 top: mariaflaya/iStockphoto; 170 bottom: Byronsdad/iStockphoto; 171 top: EcoPrint/Shutterstock; 171 center: Mary Clay/Ardea; 171 bottom: Tim Laman/National Geographic Creative; 172 left: Courtesy of Sara Ruane; 172 right: Joe Riis/National Geographic Creative; 173 top left: Don Arnold/Getty Images; 173 top right: Steven David Miller/Nature Picture Library; 173 bottom: Gregory G. Dimijian, M.D./Science Source.

Fly Guy Presents: Sharks copyright © 2013 by Tedd Arnold
Fly Guy Presents: Dinosaurs copyright © 2014 by Tedd Arnold
Fly Guy Presents: Insects copyright © 2015 by Tedd Arnold
Fly Guy Presents: Bats copyright © 2015 by Tedd Arnold
Fly Guy Presents: Snakes copyright © 2016 by Tedd Arnold

All rights reserved. Published by Scholastic Inc., *Publishers since 1920.* SCHOLASTIC and associated logos are trademarks and/or registered trademarks of Scholastic Inc.

The publisher does not have any control over and does not assume any responsibility for author or third-party websites or their content.

No part of this publication may be reproduced, stored in a retrieval system, or transmitted in any form or by any means, electronic, mechanical, photocopying, recording, or otherwise, without written permission of the publisher. For information regarding permission, write to Scholastic Inc., Attention: Permissions Department, 557 Broadway, New York, NY 10012.

ISBN 978-1-338-56590-4

10 9 8 7 6 5 4 3 2 1 20 21 22 23 24

Printed in China 62
This edition first printing, January 2020

Cover design by Sunny Lee

TABLE OF CONTENTS

A boy had a pet fly named Fly Guy.
Fly Guy could say the boy's name —

Buzz and Fly Guy were at the
aquarium (ah-KWEAR-ee-um).

"Let's go see the sharks!" said Buzz.

Fly Guy seemed scared.

"Sharks are cool!" said Buzz. "There's nothing to be afraid of here at the aquarium."

They dived in to find out more....

Scientists have found about 400 different kinds of sharks. Each shark has amazing abilities.

GRAY REEF SHARK

BLUE SHARK

LEOPARD SHARK

SPINY
DOGFISH SHARK

BASKING SHARK

PREHISTORIC
SHARK

Sharks have
been around
for over 400
million years!

PREHISTORIC
SHARK TOOTH

Sharks are fish. They live in bodies of water all over the world—even in lakes and rivers!

Like other fish, sharks breathe through gills.

GILLZZ

BULL SHARK

A shark's skeleton is made of cartilage (KAR-tuh-lij). Sharks don't have any bones.

great white shark

Cartilage makes sharks flexible. They can turn quickly to catch a bite to eat.

coral catshark

Sharks have many rows of teeth.
Only the front row is used for eating.

JAW OF A
NURSE SHARK

COOKIE-CUTTER
SHARK JAWS

The mouth of a shark can hold thousands of teeth at one time!

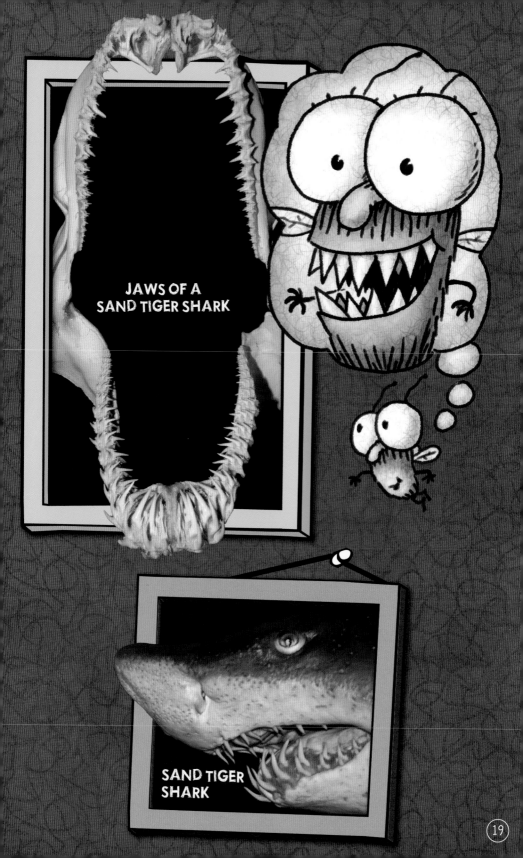

JAWS OF A
SAND TIGER SHARK

SAND TIGER
SHARK

19

Most sharks are carnivores (KAR-nih-vorz). They eat meat, such as fish and seagulls.

WHITETIP REEF SHARK

A shark uses its sharp teeth to rip its prey. Then the shark swallows the meat whole—without even chewing!

I'm hungry. How about a tuna fish sandwich?

Not all sharks eat meat.

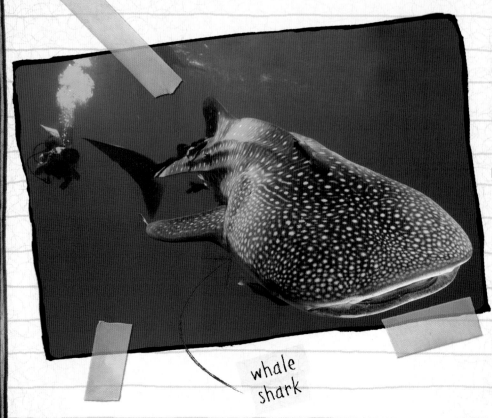

whale
shark

The whale shark is the
largest shark in the
world. It eats a small
plant called plankton
and other tiny plants.

PLANTZZ?

Close-up of plankton!

Close-up of whale-shark teeth!

...sharks have rough skin made ...les (DEN-tih-kuhlz).

BLUE SHARK

...s hard and
...Denticles
...t sharks
...arm.

A BLUE SHARK'S TINY DENTICLES

GREAT WHITE SHARK

ROUGH AND TOUGH!

A GREAT WHITE SHARK'S DENTICLES

A GREENLAND SHARK'S DENTICLES

Nurse sharks have smoother skin than most sharks. It feels like sandpaper.

Other fish have smooth, slippery scales. A shark's teeth can bite right through them.

Sharks have super senses. That makes them great hunters.

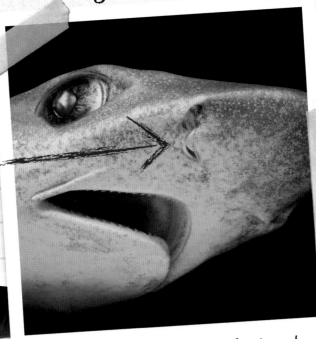

nose

Moses smoothhound shark

ear

Bigeye houndshark

A shark can hear its prey moving underwater! It can even hear a fish's muscles moving as it swims.

whitetip reef shark

LESSER SPOTTED
DOGFISH
(SMALL SPOTTED CATSHARK)

A shark has special eyesight that helps it to navigate (NAV-ih-gayt) through dark, murky water.

People need special
glasses to see in
the dark.

But a shark can feel
its prey nearby without
even seeing it!

GREAT WHITE
SHARK

Sharks are very smart. They have brains—just like humans and flies.

They have supersensitive noses to sniff out their next meal. Two-thirds of a shark's brain is used for smelling.

Many baby sharks, which are called pups, hatch from eggs. A mother shark can have up to 100 pups at a time.

A swell shark embryo within the egg.

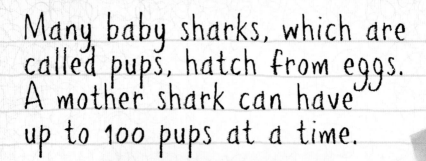

A newborn swell shark coming out of its egg case.

A newborn shark pup resting!

Most sharks live to be about 25 years old. That's way longer than the life of a fly!

A newborn lemon shark pup swimming away from its mother.

Sharks do not sleep. Most have to keep moving in order to breathe!

WHITETIP REEF SHARK

Sharks are superfast swimmers. They can move at up to 25 miles per hour! But they cannot swim backward.

GOBLIN SHARK

Some sharks are nocturnal (nok-TUR-nuhl) hunters. They are more active at night.

In the dark, a cookie-cutter shark uses a special light called luminescence (loo-mih-NEH-suhns). This light makes the shark look smaller so that its prey is not scared away. The shark surprises its prey and takes a cookie-sized bite!

COOKIE-CUTTER SHARK

This one glows in the dark!

"Wow!" said Buzz. "We learned a lot about sharks today. They are so cool!"

Fly Guy was not scared anymore.

"Fly Guy," said Buzz, "I can't wait for our next field trip!"

A boy had a pet fly named Fly Guy.
Fly Guy could say the boy's name —

Fly Guy was excited. They went inside to learn about dinosaurs. . . .

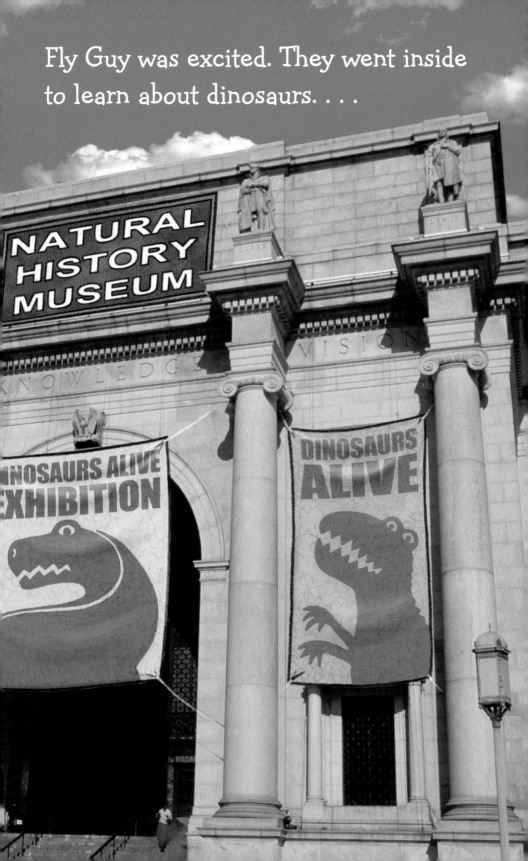

PANGAEA

Dinosaurs walked the earth about 250 million years ago, during the Mesozoic (mehz-uh-ZOH-ick) Era. Back then, all the land on Earth was pushed together. This landmass was called Pangaea (pan-GEE-uh).

THE SEVEN CONTINENTS TODAY

Dinosaurs lived all across Pangaea.

Over millions of years, the land drifted apart to form seven continents.

TRICERATOPS

BRACHIOSAURUS

Humans did not live when dinosaurs were alive. But flies did!

Scientists have discovered 700 kinds of dinosaurs! Not all dinosaurs lived at the same time.

FLYOSAURZZZ!

TYRANNOSAURUS REX

STEGOSAURUS

For example, Tyrannosaurus rex (tuh-ran-uh-SAWR-uhs reks) and Stegosaurus (steh-guh-SAWR-uhs) never met because they lived at different times.

Dinosaurs were reptiles. Reptiles are covered in scales.

Scales! →

Other reptiles include crocodiles, lizards, and turtles.

crocodile

lizard

turtle

Dinosaurs are also closely related to birds. That is because of how their leg bones join to their hips.

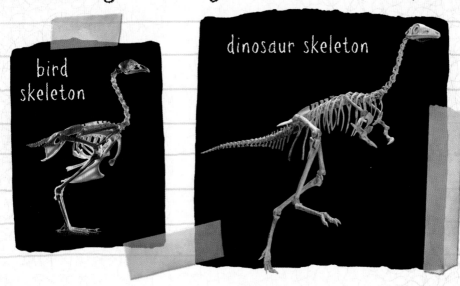

bird skeleton

dinosaur skeleton

All dinosaurs had scales, but some even had feathers, like birds.

feathered dinosaur

DINOSAUR EGG FOSSIL

HADROSAUR EGGS

DINOSAUR NEST

Baby dinosaurs hatched from eggs. Some eggs were as big as footballs. Others were small. Most dinosaur eggs were laid in nests on the ground.

CRESTED DUCKBILL DINOSAUR NEST

ALLOSAURUS

ALLOSAURUS TEETH

Some dinosaurs, such as Allosaurus (ah-loh-SAWR-uhs), ate other dinosaurs or animals. They were carnivores (CAHR-nih-vohrz). Carnivores had sharp teeth for hunting and chewing meat.

Other dinosaurs, like Iguanodon (ig-WAHN-uh-dohn), ate only plants. They were herbivores (HURB-ih-vohrz). Herbivores had flat teeth for chewing leaves.

VEGETARIANZZZ?

IGUANODONS

IGUANODON TEETH

MEAT TOOTH

VEGGIE TOOTH

Tyrannosaurus rex was a carnivore.
T. rex had sharp teeth and claws.
It could run fast, and had a good
sense of smell.

T.rex

T.rex claws

T. rex was about forty feet long.
That's as long as a school bus!

T. rex was a great hunter.
That is why T. rex is called
"king of the dinosaurs."

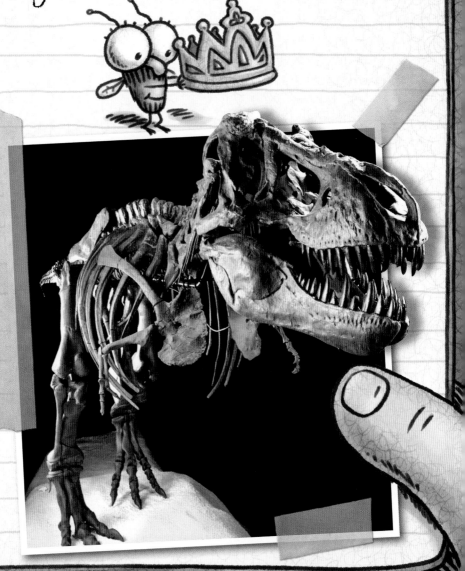

VELOCIRAPTOR CHASING PREY

Many dinosaurs, including T. rex, were predators (PREH-duh-turz). They hunted other dinosaurs or animals, called prey (PRAY). Dinosaurs had weapons to scare off predators or to hunt prey.

Many predators, like Velociraptor (veh-lohss-ih-RAHP-tur), had sharp teeth and claws.

VELOCIRAPTOR CLAW

Stegosaurus was an herbivore. It had a large, spiked tail to help keep predators away.

STEGOSAURUS TAIL

My body is my weapon!

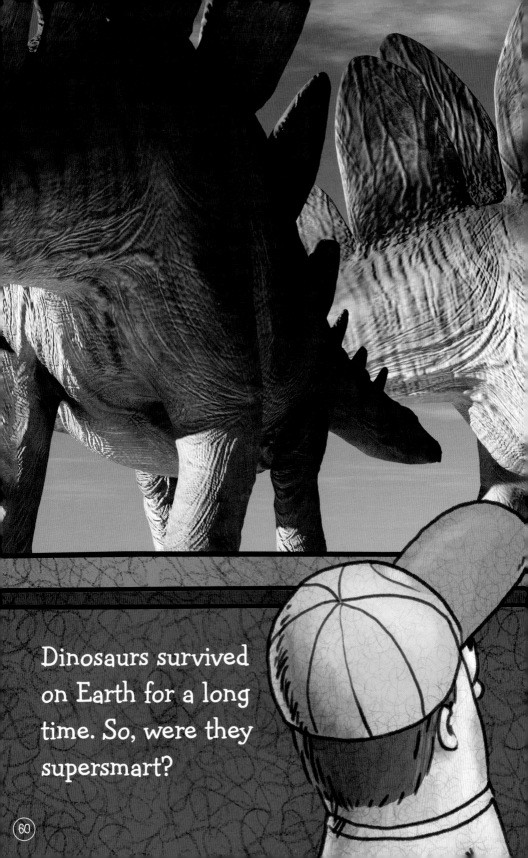

Dinosaurs survived on Earth for a long time. So, were they supersmart?

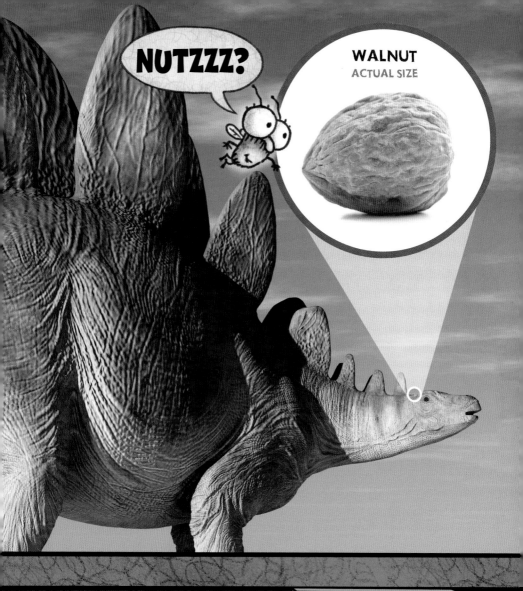

• STEGOSAURUS •

They were good hunters and defenders. But most dinosaurs were no smarter than cats or dogs. Scientists believe that most dinosaurs had small brains. Stegosaurus had a brain the size of a walnut.

Many reptiles that lived in the Mesozoic Era were not dinosaurs. Dinosaurs lived only on land.

Pterosaurs (TEH-roh-sawrz) were flying reptiles. A Pterodactyl is a type of Pterosaur.

Pterodactyls

Pterodactyl landing

Plesiosaurs (PLEH-zee-oh-sawrz) lived in water during the time dinosaurs lived.

Plesiosaur

Pterosaurs and Plesiosaurs were not dinosaurs.

Dinosaurs ruled the planet for 165 million years. But about 65 million years ago, they all died out, or became extinct (eks-TINKT) Scientists don't know why.

Some think a giant meteor hit Earth. Others think an ash cloud from a volcano's explosion blocked the sun, leaving the dinosaurs with nothing to eat.

HUMAN FOOT NEXT TO A DINOSAUR FOOTPRINT

Fossilized dinosaur poop is called coprolite (CAH-pruh-lyt).

COPROLITE

Fossils are the remains of something that existed long ago.

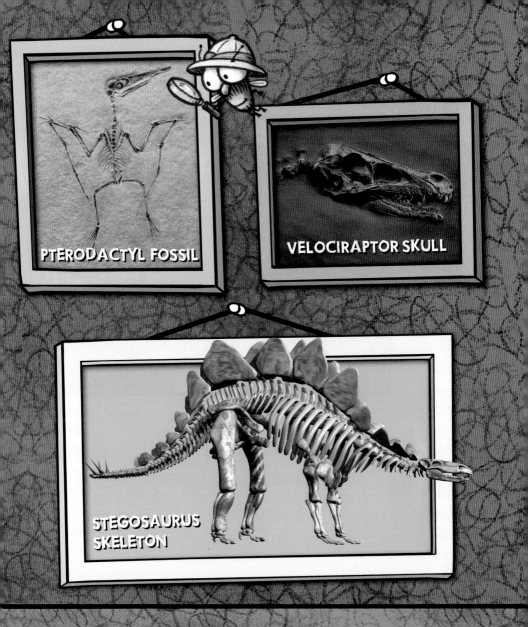

PTERODACTYL FOSSIL

VELOCIRAPTOR SKULL

STEGOSAURUS
SKELETON

They can be in rocks that formed over many years. Other fossils include dinosaur bones. Scientists have learned a lot about dinosaurs by uncovering fossils.

A paleontologist is a scientist who studies the history of life on Earth.

paleontologist in the lab

Paleontologists go on special trips called digs to look for dinosaur bones. When they find bones, they rebuild the skeleton.

Dig!

Each bone is dug up.
Then it is cleaned.

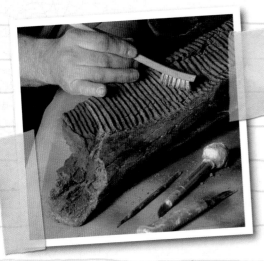

Next the scientists put the bones together like a very hard puzzle.

paleontologist building a dinosaur skeleton

Paleontologists sometimes make mistakes.... A paleontologist put the wrong skull on an Apatosaurus (ah-pat-uh-SAWR-uhs) skeleton. He thought it was a new kind of dinosaur and called it Brontosaurus (bron-tuh-SAWR-uhs) by mistake.

BISON

TRICERATOPS SKULL

In 1887, another paleontologist found a skull in Wyoming. He thought it belonged to an extinct bison. Later, he learned it belonged to Triceratops (try-SEH-ruh-topz)!

Back at home, Buzz built a skeleton.

"Dinosaurs are awesome!" he said.
"I can't wait to go on another field trip!"

INSECTS

A boy had a pet fly named Fly Guy.
Fly Guy could say the boy's name —

Buzz and Fly Guy were outside. Fly Guy wanted to look for insects. Buzz was a little worried.

"Some insects are scary," he said.

FLYZZZ?

"I know, Fly Guy, you're an insect," said Buzz. "And you are not scary. I have nothing to be afraid of."

They set off to discover more.

There are more than one million different kinds of insects!

Insects live all over the world. They live on every continent — even Antarctica!

Many people call insects bugs. But not all insects are bugs. A bug is a kind of insect. Bugs have a mouth shaped like a straw. True bugs include milkweed bugs, boxelder bugs, and stinkbugs.

• BOXELDER BUG •

• MILKWEED BUG •

• STINKBUG •

Insects have been on Earth for hundreds of millions of years. They crawled and buzzed around even before the dinosaurs.

Long ago insects were much bigger than they are today.

A giant dragonfly's wings stretched over two feet long. That's the same as the wingspan of an arctic puffin.

GIANT DRAGONFLY

ARTHROPLEURA

ARCTIC PUFFIN

LION

Arthropleura (ar-throw-PLEW-rah) was like a giant centipede. It was six feet long. That's the average length of a lion!

All insects have a life cycle. A life cycle is made up of the changes that happen to the insect from the beginning of its life until it dies.

Most insects hatch from eggs. The insect grows into a larva (LAR-vuh). Fly larvae are called maggots.

MAGGOTZ

Larvae molt, or get rid of their old skin, to grow bigger.

molting cicada

Next, the insect becomes a pupa (PEW-puh). The pupa hides in a shell, or cocoon. There, it changes into an adult. This is called metamorphosis (meht-uh-MAWR-fuh-sihs).

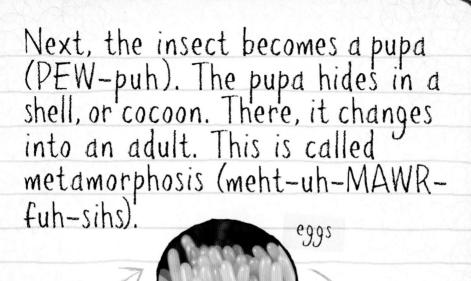

eggs

adult

METAMORPHOSIS

larvae

pupa

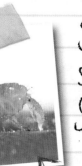

Some insects, such as aphids, give birth to live young.

aphid birth

A life span is the amount of time that a creature lives. Insects do not all have the same life span.

MAYFLY

Adult mayflies live for only one or two nights.

Some insects, such as a queen ant, can live for up to 30 years!

QUEEN ANT

ANT HILL

ANT EGGS

Insects have cool bodies! Mammals, like humans, have bones on the inside. But insects wear their hard parts on the outside. This is called an exoskeleton (ek-soh-SKEH-luh-tun).

RHINO BEETLES

An insect's body is made up of three parts: the head, the thorax, and the abdomen.

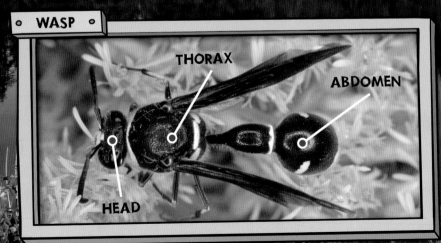

WASP

THORAX

ABDOMEN

HEAD

The head is where the eyes, mouthparts, and antennae (an-TEN-ay) are found. Antennae help insects taste, smell, touch, and even hear!

The thorax is the middle part of an insect. It holds the legs. All insects have six legs. The thorax also holds the wings, if the insect has them.

The abdomen holds the insect's stomach. If the insect has a stinger, it is found here.

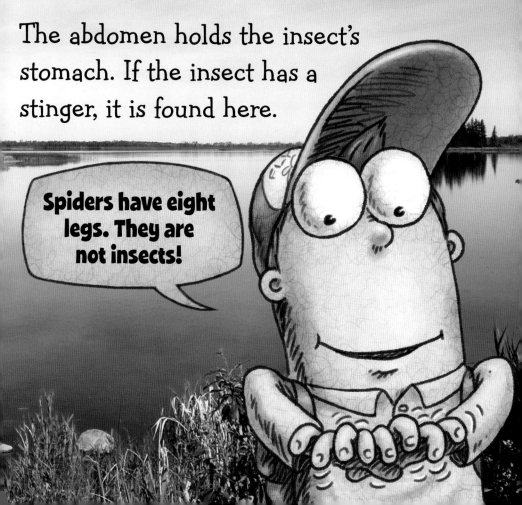

Spiders have eight legs. They are not insects!

Insects such as wasps, hornets, and some ants have stingers. Most of them use their stingers to protect themselves.

honeybee

Honeybees die after they use their stinger.

Some wasps use their stingers to catch food.

wasp

wasp stinger

hornet

STINGERZZZ!

bullet ant stinger

Usually, insects do not sting humans. But some insects will sting humans when they think they are in danger.

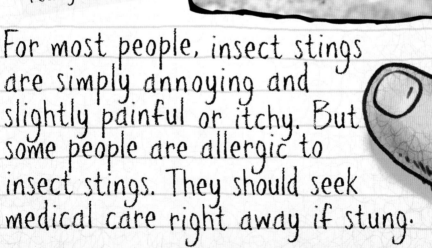

a red ant, ready to sting

For most people, insect stings are simply annoying and slightly painful or itchy. But some people are allergic to insect stings. They should seek medical care right away if stung.

Not all insects eat the same food.

Many insects munch on plants. Butterflies eat nectar (NEK-tur) from flowers.

SWALLOWTAIL BUTTERFLY

BLUE MORPHO BUTTERFLY

Other insects, such as mosquitoes, eat blood. To avoid bites, wear long sleeves and pants, and use insect repellent (rih-PEH-lunt) when outdoors.

Insects such as cockroaches and ants eat almost anything — even crumbs on the floor.

○ COCKROACHES ○

○ COCKROACH ○

Fly Guy, that's gross!

MUNCH, CRUNCH!

Insects also have different ways of eating. Some insects, like grasshoppers and caterpillars, chew their food. Other insects suck it up using a special body part called a proboscis (pro-BAHS-siss).

GRASSHOPPER

CATERPILLAR

Mosquitoes suck food up like they are drinking through a straw. The straw is the proboscis.

Some insects seem to have superpowers.

There are insects that can glow! This is called bioluminescence (by-oh-loo-mih-NEH-suhns).

fireflies

Fireflies, also called lightning bugs, are not really flies or bugs. They are beetles! They have special chemicals in their abdomens. When the chemicals meet oxygen (AHKS-ih-jen), the fireflies' abdomens light up.

Fireflies use their lights to help find other fireflies. They also light up to warn animals not to eat them—the glowing chemicals taste bad!

firefly

There are insects that can survive underwater. And some can live in very hot deserts.

diving beetle

desert locust

The world is full of amazing insects.

° FAIRYFLY °

Fairyflies are the smallest insects on Earth. These wasps can only be seen under a microscope!

The longest insect is Chan's megastick. It is 22 inches long!

Harvester ants are the most poisonous insects on the planet.

• HARVESTER ANT

• CHAN'S MEGASTICK •

In the air, the Southern giant darner dragonfly is the speediest insect. It can fly as fast as a car going 35 miles per hour!

o DARNER DRAGONFLY o

On land, the speed record goes to the cockroach. Cockroaches can run at about three and a half miles per hour.

o COCKROACH o

Cockroaches are tough. They can live for days without a head!

GUIDE BOOK TO BUGS

Flies are awesome insects!

There are 120,000 species (SPEE-sheez), or types, of flies. All flies are in the order Diptera. And a person who studies or collects flies is called a dipterist.

Flies' eyes are special — they have compound eyes. Compound eyes are not good at seeing far away. But they are great at detecting movement.

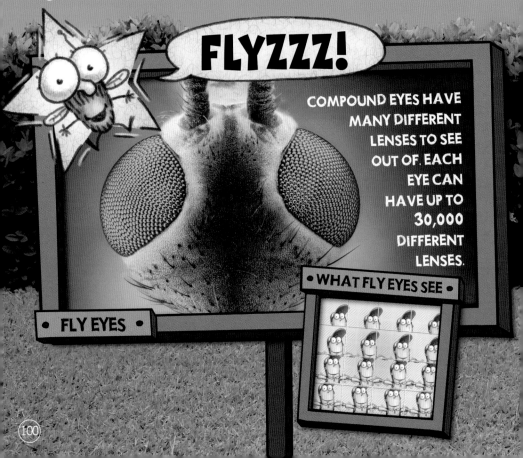

FLYZZZ!

COMPOUND EYES HAVE MANY DIFFERENT LENSES TO SEE OUT OF. EACH EYE CAN HAVE UP TO 30,000 DIFFERENT LENSES.

• WHAT FLY EYES SEE •

• FLY EYES •

If something gets close, a fly can plan an escape route in less than one second!

Most flies don't bite animals. But some flies, like deerflies and horseflies, do. They drink blood.

Flies sleep a lot! They sleep between nine and 15 hours each night.

DEERFLY

A fly's wings beat 200 times per second.

Scientists who study insects are called entomologists (en-tuh-MAHL-uh-jists).

entomologists at work

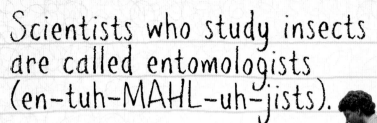

Entomologists sometimes go on expeditions (ex-puh-DIH-shunz), or special trips to look for insects. They study insects where they live. And they live everywhere!

Insects live in treetops, in hot deserts, underground, on animals, and even in frozen Antarctica.

IN JARZ TOO!

Millions of insects live in tropical rain forests. Most of them live in the canopy layer, or the tops of trees. As many as 1,000 different types of insects have been found in just <u>one</u> tree in a rain forest canopy!

canopy layer

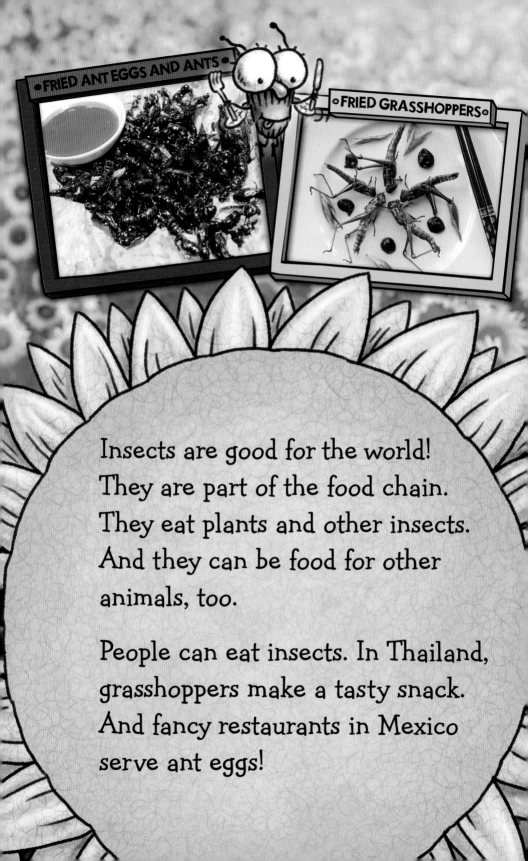

●FRIED ANT EGGS AND ANTS●

●FRIED GRASSHOPPERS●

Insects are good for the world!
They are part of the food chain.
They eat plants and other insects.
And they can be food for other
animals, too.

People can eat insects. In Thailand,
grasshoppers make a tasty snack.
And fancy restaurants in Mexico
serve ant eggs!

Insects are important to us! Plants would not be able to grow without them.

When insects, such as bees and butterflies, land on flowers, they pollinate (PAH-lih-nayt) them. Only then can fruits and vegetables grow.

• BEE POLLINATING A CHERRY TREE •

• BEES ON HONEYCOMB •

Bees also make honey. Yum!

"Insects are great!" said Buzz. "I didn't know they were so amazing."

Now Buzz knew for sure that Fly Guy was the coolest pet on the planet!

Buzz and Fly Guy couldn't wait for their next adventure.

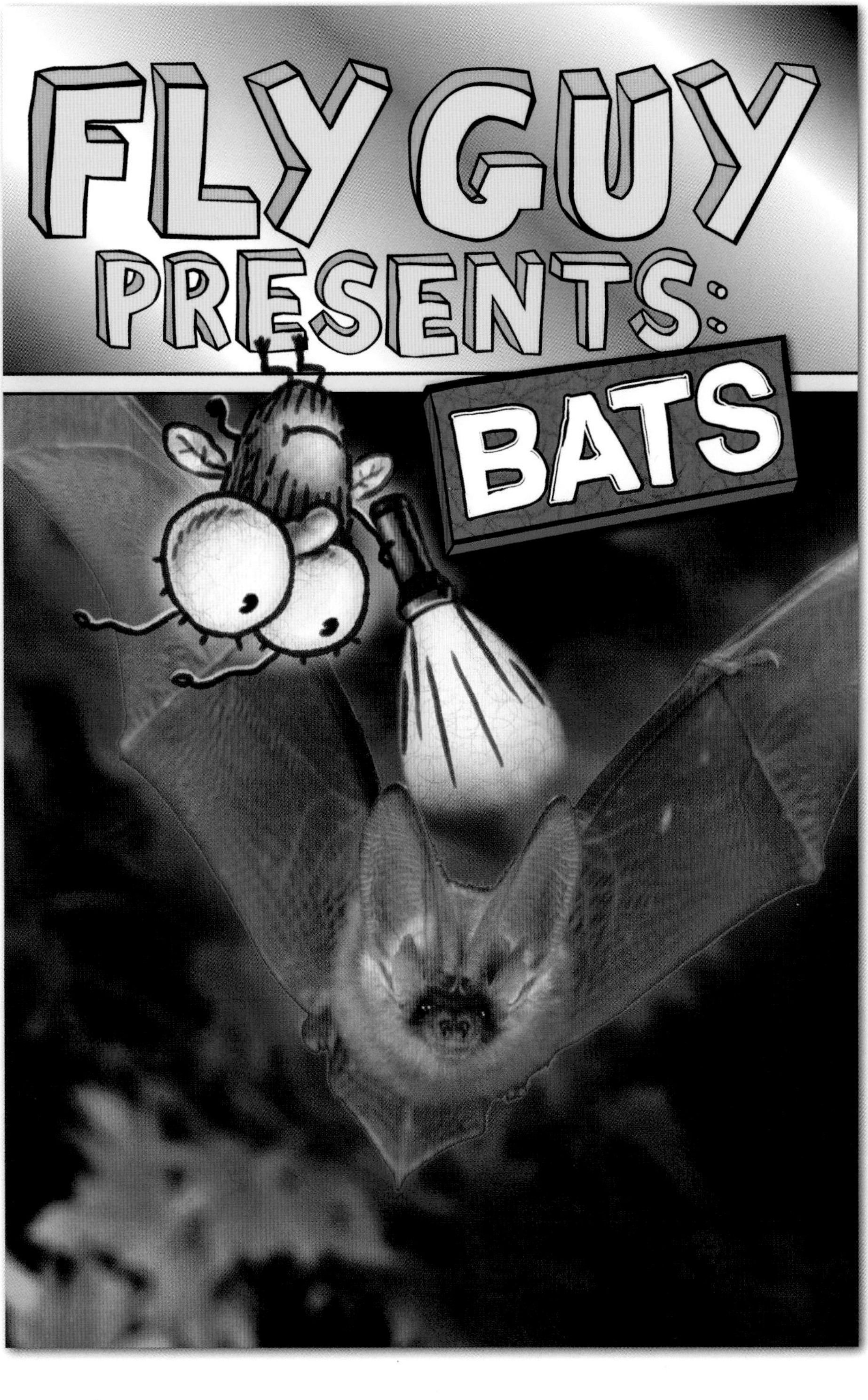
FLY GUY
PRESENTS:
BATS

A boy had a pet fly named Fly Guy.
Fly Guy could say the boy's name —

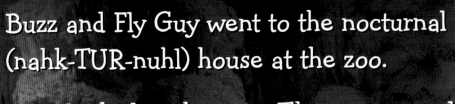

Buzz and Fly Guy went to the nocturnal (nahk-TUR-nuhl) house at the zoo.

Buzz looked at the map. They were inside a bat cave!

"Bats are so cool," said Buzz. "But I don't know much about them."

Buzz and Fly Guy wanted to learn more.

Almost all bats are nocturnal. That means they are active at night and asleep during the day.

GREATER FLYING FOX BATS SLEEPING IN TREES

Bats fly at night!

Other animals, such as raccoons and barn owls, are also mainly nocturnal.

Bats hang upside down to sleep. They hang in high places to be safe from hunting animals.

Some bats hang from trees or under bridges. Bats might even hang out in your attic!

• FRUIT BAT IN A TREE •

• LONG-EARED BATS IN ATTIC •

Other bats live in caves. They hang from the ceiling.

LESSER LONG-NOSED BATS

A group of bats is called a colony. Some colonies in caves have more than 20 million bats!

BAT COLONY IN CAVE

CAN YOU HANG LIKE A BAT?

EAZZY!

There are more than 1,200 different species (SPEE-sheez), or kinds, of bats!

tube-nosed bat

ghost bat

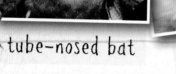

Jamaican fruit-eating bat

The most common bat in North America is the little brown bat.

little brown bat

Bats live on every continent— except for Antarctica.

the seven continents

They can be found as far north as the Arctic Circle, where temperatures can dip as low as negative 30 degrees Fahrenheit!

icy cave

They also live in very hot places, like Death Valley, California, where the temperature once reached 134 degrees Fahrenheit!

Death Valley

GREATER
FLYING FOX BAT
COAT OF FUR

Bats are mammals (MA-muhlz). Mammals
have fur and they are warm-blooded. That
means that the temperature of their bodies
does not change with the temperature of
where they are.

Bats are the only mammals in the world that can fly!

• GREATER FLYING FOX BAT COLONY •

I FLYZZ!

Yes, but you are not a mammal. You are an insect.

Flying is hard work! Bats use gravity (GRAH-vih-tee), or the force that pulls objects downward to Earth, to help them take off.

INDIAN FLYING FOX BAT

FRINGE-LIPPED BATS

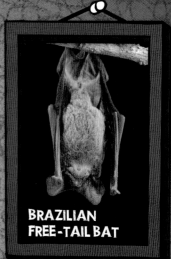

BRAZILIAN FREE-TAIL BAT

First, bats hang upside down. Next, they drop from their perch and flap their wings until they are flying through the air.

TOWNSEND'S BIG-EARED BAT IN STAGES OF FLIGHT

Most bats are small and weigh less than two ounces. That is less than an orange!

scientist holding a ghost bat

Kitti's hog-nosed bat, also called the bumblebee bat, is the world's smallest bat. It is only about one inch long.

bumblebee bat being handled by a scientist

1 INCH

There are some large bats, too. The greater flying fox bat is the largest bat in the world. From tip to tip, its wings stretch to about five feet!

greater flying fox bat soaring through the sky

5-foot-long wingspan!

Different kinds of bats eat different things.

Many bats, such as the Egyptian slit-faced bat, eat insects. Some insect-eating bats also eat frogs, lizards, small birds, and even fish!

PALLID BAT

EGYPTIAN
SLIT-FACED BAT

EATZZ
INSECTZZ?

I was hoping you
would miss that fact.

Fruit bats munch on fruits and drink nectar from flowers.

EGYPTIAN FRUIT BAT

PALLAS'S LONG-TONGUED BAT

○ FRUIT BATS FEEDING ○

• VAMPIRE BAT •

Vampire bats eat only blood. They drink from other animals, such as cattle. These bats use heat sensors to help them find the animal they are hunting.

Bats have amazing bodies.

LONG-EARED BAT SKELETON

These small mammals have two wings, two legs, and a tail. They cannot run because their legs are too small. And their wings are not as strong as a bird's.

Bats have two thumbs—one at each wrist. These thumbs help them to climb, fight, and hunt.

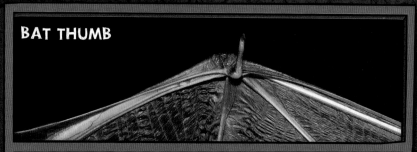

BAT THUMB

All bats have teeth. Fruit-eating bats have simpler teeth than bats that eat insects. Insect-eating bats have sharper teeth that help them crush insects. Vampire bats have razor-sharp teeth!

NICEFORO'S FOREST BAT

VAMPIRE BAT

Bats have super senses!

Some bats can see really well in the dark.

fringe-lipped bat

Bats' noses have extra-special smell sensors!

red flying fox bat

And bats have great hearing. They can hear an insect's beating wings!

WINGZZ MAKE NOIZE!

long-eared bat hunting a moth

grey long-eared bat

Many types of bats use a special sound to get around and to find food. This is called echolocation (eh-koh-loh-KAY-shun).

Bats send this sound out from their nose or mouth.

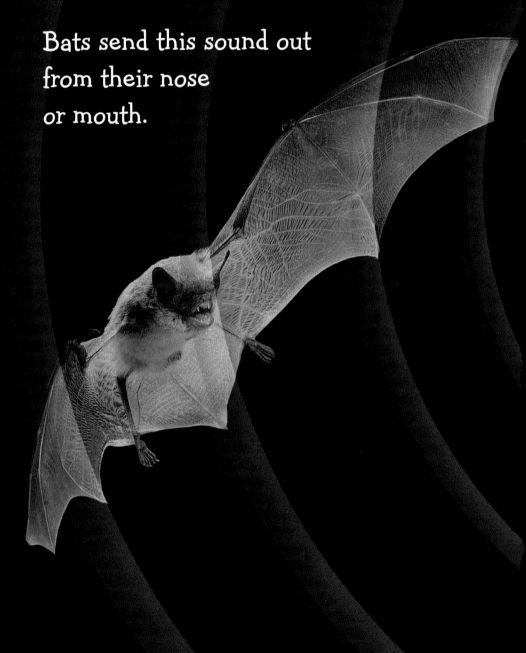

The sound travels to an object, bounces off it, and travels back to the bat's ears. This lets the bat know how far away the object is—so the bat can locate it.

Bat sounds are too high-pitched for people to hear.

Some bats make sounds louder than 110 decibels!

Not all bats hunt the same way.

Some bats, like the diadem roundleaf bat, wait for an insect to fly by. They then fly after the insect to catch it.

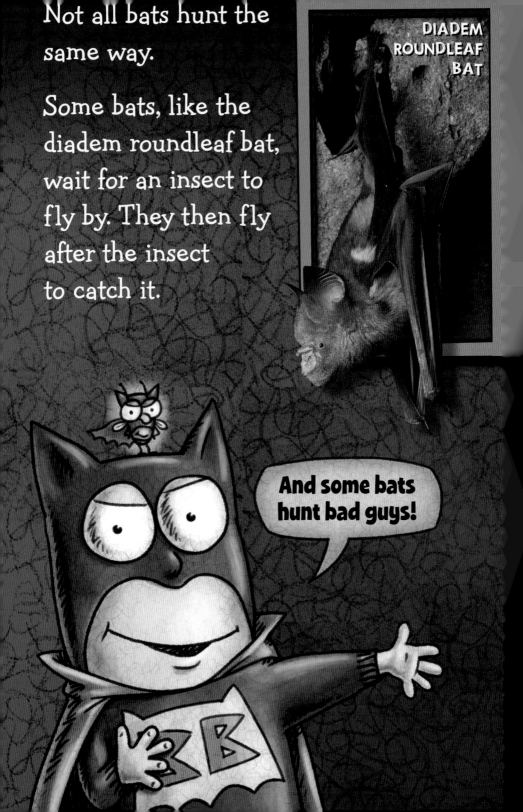

DIADEM ROUNDLEAF BAT

And some bats hunt bad guys!

Other bats hunt as a group. They help one another catch prey.

○ COLONY LEAVING CAVE ○

Many bats hibernate (HY-bur-nayt) in the winter when there is not much food. They go into a deep sleep. Then, when spring comes, the bats wake up to hunt again.

○ LITTLE BROWN BATS HIBERNATING ○

Most female bats give birth to only one baby each year. Baby bats are called pups.

PUPZZZ!

grey bat pup

All pups—even baby vampire bats—drink milk from their mothers.

Gambian bat mother and pup

Baby bats hang on to their mothers.

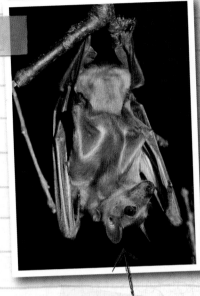

mother bats with pups

A mother bat recognizes her pup's scent and cry. Even with hundreds of pups in one colony, Mom can always find her baby.

fruit bat mother and pup

Chiropterologists (ki-RAHP-tur-AHL-uh-jists) are scientists who study bats. They try to learn more about bats.

CHIROPTEROLOGIST HOLDING A PALLID BAT CAPTURED IN A MIST NET

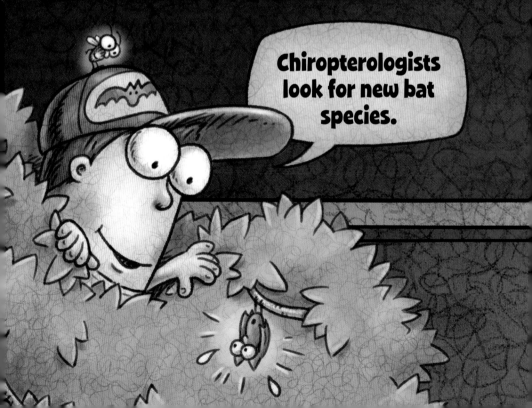

Chiropterologists look for new bat species.

DISK

In 2013, scientists discovered a new species of disk-wing bat. These bats have disks on their thumbs that help them to climb.

"Bats are amazing!" said Buzz. "From now on, I promise to never try to swat a bat, even if one gets in my house. I will get help to safely remove it. Bats are our friends."

Buzz and Fly Guy couldn't wait for their next adventure.

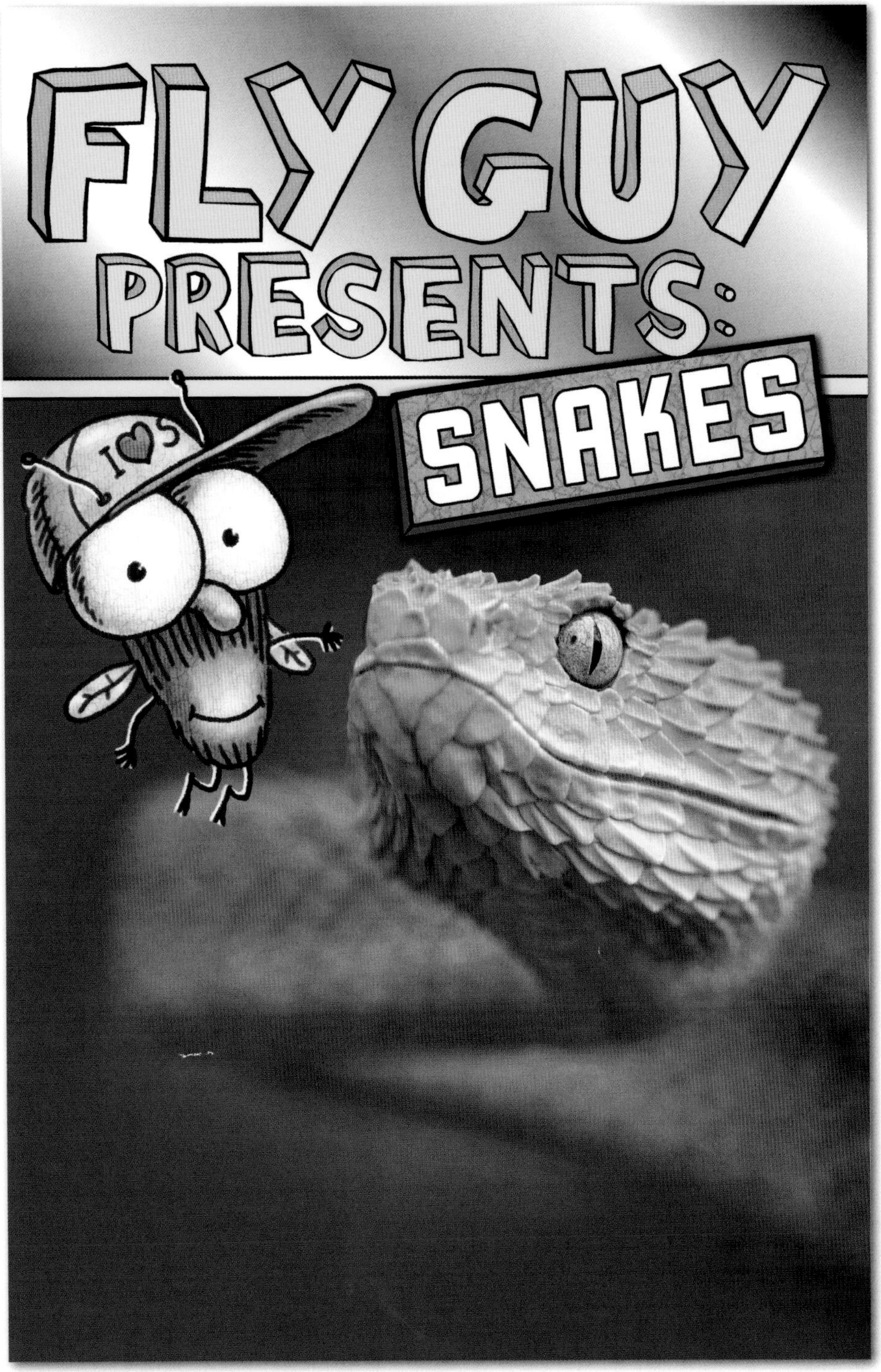
FLY GUY
PRESENTS:
SNAKES
I ♥ S

A boy had a pet fly named Fly Guy.
Fly Guy could say the boy's name —

BUZZ!

"I know where to find snakes at the zoo," said Buzz. "Look! It's the Snake House!"

Fly Guy was curious.

Snakes aren't as scary as people think, said Buzz. "Let's find out more!"

They opened the door and stepped inside . . .

Snakes are reptiles. Lizards, turtles, and crocodiles are reptiles, too.

HORNED LIZARD

CROCODILE

TURTLE

All reptiles have scaly skin, lungs for breathing, and backbones.

• SNAKE SKELETON •

Reptiles are ectotherms (ek-toe-therms). They cannot create their own body heat. They need sunlight to warm their bodies.

RED-TAILED RATSNAKE

It looks like this snake is having fun in the sun!

Scales protect a snake's body and help it move. Scales are made of keratin—the same material as human fingernails!

MATILDA'S
HORNED VIPER

SIDEWINDER

Some snakes' scales grip the ground like tire treads. Then muscles help them slither forward.

As a snake grows, it sheds its skin. It sheds all of its scales—even those covering its eyes! The new skin underneath looks bright and shiny.

CORN SNAKE SHEDDING

BOA CONSTRICTOR SHEDDING

Many snakes use the color and texture of their scaly skin to make it harder for other animals to see them. This is called camouflage (KAM-uh-flahzh).

BUZZ?

There are more than 3,000 kinds of snakes in the world.

tree python

cobra

Cope's
vine snake

mangrove
snake

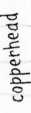

copperhead

bushmaster

Snakes live on every continent except Antarctica.

long-nosed snake

NORTH
AMERICA

EUROPE

ASIA

AFRICA

SOUTH
AMERICA

AUSTRALIA

ANTARCTICA

the seven continents

Most snakes live on land. Snakes can live almost anywhere — in grasslands, wetlands, deserts, forests, swamps, trees, and caves. Some snakes even live in the ocean!

diamondback rattlesnake

green pit viper

All snakes can swim, but sea snakes have flat tails. These special tails make it easier for them to move through water.

olive sea snake

check out its flat tail!

Humans have five senses — sight, hearing, taste, smell, and touch. Snake senses are similar, but snakes sometimes use different body parts for these functions.

Snakes have two eyes but no eyelids. Most snakes can only see what is right in front of them, and it is often blurry. A clear scale called a brille (BRILL-a) covers each eye for protection.

Snakes never close their eyes!

Snakes do not have external ears. They do not hear sounds the same way as humans. They feel sounds as vibrations (vi-BRAY-shuns) in their bodies.

NO EARZZ!

AFRICAN BUSH VIPER

Snakes use their nostrils to breathe, not to smell. They have forked tongues that help them taste AND smell.

Snakes flick out their tongues to pick up chemicals in the air. The taste of these chemicals tells them food is nearby.

NORTHERN BLACK-TAILED RATTLESNAKE

Snakes' scales allow them to feel the texture of things they slither over, like sand, dirt, grass, or water.

BURMESE PYTHON

KING COBRA

NORTH AMERICAN WATER SNAKE

Some snakes have a sixth sense.

Pit vipers have special organs called pits between each eye and nostril. These pits allow the snake to see the body heat of animals nearby. That means pit vipers—such as rattlesnakes—can hunt in the dark!

Mojave rattlesnake

HUNTZ FLYZZ?

black-tailed rattlesnake

snake "pit"

Pythons and boas also have pits. Their pits are located on the lips and lower jaw. These snakes sense the heat of nearby animals.

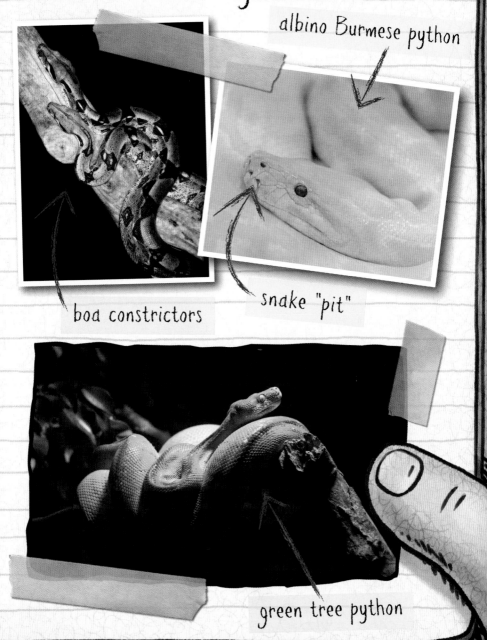

albino Burmese python

boa constrictors

snake "pit"

green tree python

Snakes have lived on Earth for about 140 million years.

The largest snake ever discovered was the Titanoboa. It weighed around 2,500 pounds.

● TITANOBOA WAS MORE THAN 40 FEET LONG ●

Titanoboa lived around 58 million years ago. That's 5 million years after T. rex roamed the earth, but this prehistoric giant was just as scary!

● T. REX ●

The largest snake alive today is the green anaconda. Most anacondas grow as long as a pickup truck. Some can be even longer!

GREEN ANACONDA

The smallest snake is the Barbados threadsnake. It is less than four inches long.

CUTE-ZIE!

BARBADOS THREADSNAKE

Snakes eat and kill other animals, called prey (PRAY). Snakes can eat small mammals, birds, fish, worms, and even other reptiles or snakes.

DICE SNAKE

Some snakes, like boas and pythons, are constrictors. They coil their bodies around their prey and squeeze until the animal stops breathing.

BOA CONSTRICTOR SQUEEZING PREY

he bottom of a snake's jaw is loosely attached to the snake's skull rather than to the top jaw. This allows a snake to open its mouth wide enough to swallow the animal whole.

BALL PYTHON

COMMON EGG-EATING SNAKE

Could a snake swallow me?!

Many snakes, like cobras, mambas, vipers, and rattlesnakes, bite their prey. The snake's sharp fangs shoot a deadly poison called venom (VEN-uhm) into the animal's body.

yellow eyelash viper biting Gecko

The poison weakens, paralyzes, or kills the animal. Then the snake swallows it whole.

African house snake digesting prey

Great Lakes bush viper

FLYZZ BITEZ TOO!

Sometimes snakes bite humans. Many snake bites can be treated with a special medicine called antivenom (AN-tee-ven-uhm). Antivenom helps the body defend itself from the poison.

scientists use snake venom to create antivenom

About three-quarters of the world's snakes lay soft, leathery eggs. These snakes are oviparous (oh-VIP-er-uhs).

EASTERN HOGNOSE SNAKES

BABYZZ!

Fly Guy, they may not like milk.

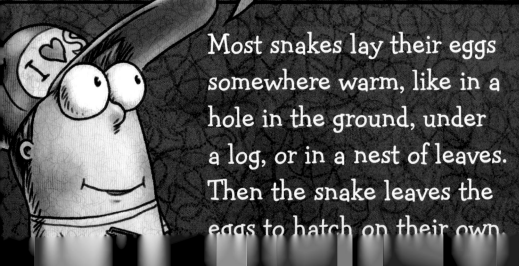

Most snakes lay their eggs somewhere warm, like in a hole in the ground, under a log, or in a nest of leaves. Then the snake leaves the eggs to hatch on their own.

but other snakes—like the python and the king cobra—stick around to warm or protect their eggs.

ANGOLAN PYTHON

Not all snakes lay eggs. Viviparous (vie-VIP-er-uhs) snakes give birth to live babies. Anacondas, many sea snakes, and most vipers are viviparous.

NEWBORN COPPERHEADS WITH MOTHER

Rattlesnakes have special hard pieces on their tails. These hard pieces are made of keratin, the same material as snake scales. When a rattlesnake shakes its tail, these pieces vibrate and create a rattling sound. This sound warns predators to stay back.

Way to shake, rattle, and roll!

Every time a rattlesnake sheds its skin, it grows another piece on its tail. But don't try to guess a rattlesnake's age by counting its rattles! Snakes can shed a few times a year, and rattle pieces can break off easily.

MIDGET FADED RATTLESNAKE

Some snakes live just a few years in the wild. Others can live to be more than 25 years old!

People believe many things about snakes. Some of these things are true, but some are false.

TRUE OR FALSE?

1. A snake can grab its tail in its mouth and roll after prey. FALSE! A stressed snake may bite its own tail by mistake. But "hoop snakes" are not real.

2. Snakes can hypnotize people. FALSE! They look like they are staring because they don't have eyelids.

3. Snakes dance to music. **FALSE!** A snake might look like it's dancing because it can sometimes follow the movements of a flute.

4. Snakes hiss. **TRUE!** Some snakes can push air through an organ in their throats. This makes a hissing sound.

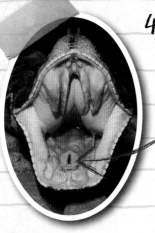

5. Flying snakes are real. **TRUE!** (sort of) Some tree-climbing snakes can push off into the air and glide down to the ground.

A scientist who studies snakes is called a herpetologist (hur-puh-TAH-luh-jist).

HERPETOLOGIST HOLDING A BLUNT-HEADED TREE SNAKE

HERPETOLOGIST HOLDING A PIT VIPER

Some herpetologists study toxic snake venom and hope to use it to create cures for human diseases. Someday, venom that makes it hard for animals to stop bleeding could help save someone who is having a heart attack!

Other herpetologists work at zoos or museums. They teach people about snakes and other reptiles.

BOA CONSTRICTOR

We sure learned a lot!

DUMERIL'S BOA

"Wow!" said Buzz. "I had no idea just how cool snakes really are!"

Buzz and Fly Guy could not wait for their next field trip.

FLY GUY PRESENTS

Go on field trips with Fly Guy!
A nonfiction series filled with fun facts and cool photos!

FLY GUY PRESENTS: SPACE
Tedd Arnold
SCHOLASTIC

FLY GUY PRESENTS: DINOSAURS
Tedd Arnold
SCHOLASTIC

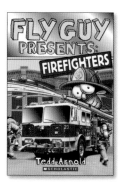

FLY GUY PRESENTS: FIREFIGHTERS
Tedd Arnold
SCHOLASTIC

FLY GUY PRESENTS: INSECTS
Tedd Arnold
SCHOLASTIC

FLY GUY PRESENTS: BATS
Tedd Arnold
SCHOLASTIC

FLY GUY PRESENTS: SNAKES
Tedd Arnold
SCHOLASTIC

FLY GUY PRESENTS: THE WHITE HOUSE
Tedd Arnold
SCHOLASTIC

FLY GUY PRESENTS: WEATHER
Tedd Arnold
SCHOLASTIC

FLY GUY PRESENTS: CASTLES
Tedd Arnold
SCHOLASTIC

FLY GUY PRESENTS POLICE OFFICERS
Tedd Arnold
SCHOLASTIC

FLY GUY PRESENTS GARBAGE & RECYCLING
Tedd Arnold
SCHOLASTIC

FLY GUY PRESENTS MONSTER TRUCKS
Tedd Arnold
SCHOLASTIC

Art © 2017 by Tedd Arnold.
SCHOLASTIC and associated logos are trademarks
and/or registered trademarks of Scholastic Inc.

SCHOLASTIC
scholastic.com

FGPRES13